SOCIAL WORKER

BY STEPHANIE FINNE

T0014874

BLUE OWL
BOOKS

TIPS FOR CAREGIVERS

Social and emotional learning (SEL) helps children manage emotions, create and achieve goals, maintain relationships, learn how to feel empathy, and make good decisions. The SEL approach will help children establish positive habits in communication, cooperation, and decision-making. By incorporating SEL in early reading, children will be better equipped to build confidence and foster positive peer networks.

BEFORE READING

Talk to the reader about different struggles people face.

Discuss: What difficulties have you seen in your family? Have your friends faced hard times? What about people in your community or town?

AFTER READING

Talk to the reader about social work and empathy.

Discuss: What does a social worker do? How does a social worker help others?

SEL GOAL

Some students may struggle with social awareness, making it hard to empathize with others. Help readers stop and think about others. How can they help someone who is going through a hard time? What can helping others do for them? How can it help the community? Discuss how learning to do these things can help them develop empathy.

TABLE OF CONTENTS

CHAPTER 1

WHAT IS A SOCIAL WORKER?

Social workers help people work through problems and improve their lives. How? They offer **counseling** and support. They help people find **resources**.

Social workers aid people of all ages. They talk with and help individuals, families, or groups. They work in many settings. These include schools, hospitals, and prisons.

CHAPTER 2

BECOMING A SOCIAL WORKER

To become a social worker, you must get a four-year college degree in the field. Then, you complete an **internship**. An experienced social worker trains you. You must pass an exam to get a **license**. Some social workers also get a **master's degree**.

Social workers are good listeners. They **empathize** and provide counseling. They find out what each **client** needs. Together, they create goals.

Social workers can connect clients with more resources. When John was lonely, he went to the senior center. A social worker there helped him make a plan to meet people. John decided to join a chess club. He made friends!

Matt is a social worker in a clinic for **veterans**. Paula wants to find a new job. Matt listens to what Paula wants to do. Then, he helps her look.

SOCIAL WORKER TRAITS

Social workers are organized.
They are patient and understanding.
They are good at solving problems.

CHAPTER 3

TYPES OF SOCIAL WORKERS

School social workers help students. Allie has been getting in fights at school. A school social worker helps Allie learn to pause and be **mindful** of her emotions.

School social workers might talk to students' families. They may work with teachers and staff, too. This helps them understand how to best help students.

Adrian is in **foster care**. A social worker checks on him and his foster family. The social worker makes sure he is safe. He learns that Adrian is **depressed**. He connects him with a **therapist** for more counseling.

HOME VISITS

Social workers may visit people in their homes. Why? This can help them understand how a person or family is doing in their everyday life.

Hospital social workers build relationships between patients and their medical team. They often help with planning for when a patient leaves the hospital. They make sure the patient will be safe at home.

Ty has **diabetes**. A hospital social worker helped Ty's family fill out paperwork. She also helped them get questions answered by Ty's doctors and nurses.

Some social workers help people who do not have a home. Others work with people who struggle with **substance use**. There are also social workers who work with military families.

HOW MANY MEETINGS?

A social worker may meet with a client just once or several times. It depends on how long the person needs help.

Social workers help wherever they are needed. They do important work. Would you like to be a social worker?

GOALS AND TOOLS

GROW WITH GOALS

Social workers must be able to empathize with others. Try working on these goals.

Goal: Listen to someone tell a story. Think about how you would feel if it was happening to you.

Goal: Ask a friend or classmate a question. Listen to their answer and think about how they are feeling.

Goal: List four ways you can help someone else.

TRY THIS!

Try this breathing exercise to help you focus and calm yourself. First, close your eyes. Imagine a cup of hot cocoa. Pretend to hold and smell the cocoa. Breathe in through your nose as you count to five. Then, blow on the hot cocoa to cool it off as you count to five again. Repeat this until you feel calm.

GLOSSARY

client
A person who uses services and gets advice from a professional.

counseling
Advice.

depressed
A medical condition in which you feel unhappy, irritated, or hopeless, can't concentrate or sleep well, and aren't interested in activities you normally enjoy.

diabetes
A long-term medical condition that affects blood sugar.

empathize
Understanding and sharing the emotions and experiences of another.

foster care
Temporary care for a person in a home setting.

internship
A practice in which a student gains supervised experience in a professional field.

license
A permit or permission granted by a group to do something.

master's degree
A degree given by a college or university usually after one or two years of additional study following a bachelor's degree.

mindful
Focused on the present moment and calmly recognizing and accepting your feelings, thoughts, and sensations.

resources
People, places, or things that can help someone deal with a difficult situation.

substance use
Use of drugs or alcohol.

therapist
A health-care worker who is trained to treat people dealing with mental or physical issues.

veterans
People who used to serve in the military.

TO LEARN MORE

FACT SURFER

Finding more information is as easy as 1, 2, 3.

1. Go to www.factsurfer.com
2. Enter "**socialworker**" into the search box.
3. Choose your book to see a list of websites.

INDEX

Blue Owl Books are published by Jump!, 5357 Penn Avenue South, Minneapolis, MN 55419, www.jumplibrary.com

Copyright © 2024 Jump! International copyright reserved in all countries. No part of this book may be reproduced in any form without written permission from the publisher.

Library of Congress Cataloging-in-Publication Data

Names: Finne, Stephanie, author.
Title: Social worker / by Stephanie Finne.
Description: Minneapolis, MN: Jump!, Inc., [2024]
Series: SEL careers | Includes index.
Audience: Ages 7–10
Identifiers: LCCN 2023001900 (print)
LCCN 2023001901 (ebook)
ISBN 9798885246408 (hardcover)
ISBN 9798885246415 (paperback)
ISBN 9798885246422 (ebook)
Subjects: LCSH: Social workers–Juvenile literature. | Social service–Juvenile literature.
Classification: LCC HV40.35 .F56 2024 (print)
LCC HV40.35 (ebook)
DDC 361.3/2023–dc23/eng/20230124
LC record available at https://lccn.loc.gov/2023001900
LC ebook record available at https://lccn.loc.gov/2023001901

Editor: Eliza Leahy
Designer: Molly Ballanger
Content Consultant: Megan Kraemer, MSW, LICSW

Photo Credits: sturti/iStock, cover, 4; DGLimages/iStock, 1; Mega Pixel/Shutterstock, 3; Marmaduke St. John/Alamy, 5; aldomurillo/iStock, 6; SDI Productions/iStock, 7, 10–11; LightField Studios/Shutterstock, 8–9; SolStock/iStock, 12; Media_Photos/Shutterstock, 13; SeventyFour/iStock, 14–15; bluecinema/iStock, 16–17; Martinns/iStock, 18–19; Drazen Zigic/iStock, 20–21.

Printed in the United States of America at Corporate Graphics in North Mankato, Minnesota.